MW01235647

A GIRL'S GUIDE
TO STYLE THERAPY

Live it your 51%

8 Tips For Balancing Mental Health
Through Style Embracement

Felicia Baxley

Copyright © 2022 by Felicia Baxley.

All rights reserved. No part of this publication may be reproduced, distributed or transmitted in any form or by any means, including photocopying, recording, or other electronic or mechanical methods, without the prior written permission of the publisher, except in the case of brief quotations embodied in critical reviews and certain other noncommercial uses permitted by copyright law. For permission requests, write to the publisher, addressed "Attention: Permissions Coordinator," at the address below.

Hustle Write Publications LLC

Jacksonville, NC 28546

Ordering Information:

Quantity sales. Special discounts are available on quantity purchases by corporations, associations, and others. For details, contact the "Special Sales Department" at contact@pearlmae.co

A Girl's Guide to Style Therapy / Felicia Baxley—1st ed.

ISBN 978-1-73541-403-4

Table of Contents

Hey Friend,

So listen, I want to assume that you already know me, but I also wanna leave room for God to be God and get this book into the hands of everyone who may need it. That being said, I am Felicia, however most at this point know me as Pearl Mae. About two or so months ago, as I write this that is, I embarked on a journey that I couldn't have fathomed would be so rewarding. I started a TikTok. And, I mean, since it is my book and all, let's get into that for a second.

It didn't really start with a TikTok. It started with a business idea that quickly became a massive vision. Writing the details, new things constantly consuming my mind, I was quickly, and slowly, becoming a better person with an excitement to do something much bigger with my own struggles. For those of you already following my on the good ole TikyTok, you know the business in question is Style Sain d'Esprit. I hit up a friend to go over the vision for the business and get her input because I wanted to make sure I did it right.

"You should start a TikTok."

"Mmmmmm."

"I want you to come from behind the pictures. Your pictures are great but you need to start sharing your story with others. I want you to do a video this weekend."

I took that advice, and two months later I had amassed almost 30k followers, supporting me, being inspired by me, ready to follow my endeavors. Little ole me.

See, Style Sain d'Esprit, which is already registered and copyright is in processed for the weirdos that don't come up with their own ideas, isn't just going to be a clothing brand, but it's going to be a safe space that is the catalyst for women of all races, ethnicities, sizes, and ages to embrace their own personal sense of style while learning to love themselves and take care of their mental health. Just to give a quick overview in the form of a mouthful.

Creating content was easier than I thought, it didn't require any effort whatsoever, at least in the beginning. But there were still so many things I was reserved about. I had personally seen how posting things on the Internet had caused the demise of so many people, especially given the tense political climate the last couple years. Not that I'm controversial or anything, but I wanted to be able to keep the things I did on my personal time online just that, online. To date, my Internet friends still don't know my real name, though I'm sure I'll let them know by the time this book is released. This means, I haven't taken advantage of my following to promote my other books, but I was okay with that. I wanted to get to know my new friends, and I wanted them to get to know me without all the internet detective work because the reality is, sometimes people can feel entitled to the life of a creator when that's just not the case. At least not for me baby.

I remember changing my name on Facebook to reflect my other social media accounts, y'know to keep things private that I wanted to keep private. My mom texted me, "How did you come up with PearlMae?"

"Well, my friends gave me the name Pearl because they said I'm like one of those old, harsh church mothers."

I guess Pearl was the best they could come up with without giving me an older sounding name like Hattie or something. Mae just came along with it because in the south, well all the old ladies have multiple first names, and Mae is just the one I like.

4

Just yesterday one of the ladies at church said, "Felicia, girl I was seeing this PearlMae everywhere, and I was like WHO IS THIS? I finally clicked on it, it was you! I been trying to find you on TikTok because I heard you were doing prayers." I've come to enjoy it, and even after my friends know my name, I'll still be PearlMae.

@pearlmae_ on TikTok (and now YouTube) is a platform that shares my personal struggles with anxiety and depression as well as how I cope with it using my, unique, sense of style, oh and can't forget a few occasional prayers and biblical revelations because, you know: God. If you aren't already following me, you should check it out, I'm pretty dope if I do say so myself. No bias intended.

All that being said, so many have asked questions that I try my best to answer, but then I remembered: Babygirl, you're an author, write your friends a book. So that's exactly what I'm doing. When you become an author, all the research tells you to have a fan base, a social media following in this day in age, which I never necessarily had before. I'm sure by the time this book is actually published, all my internet friends will probably already know about my other books, but this one is probably the most personal yet. My passion for this is different, and I have already been amazed at the people who have taken the time to support me. More importantly, I'm blessed to know how much little ole me inspires others.

So this book, friends, is for us. Throughout this book I'm going to share some of the tips I have, in detail, to learning how to cope with mental illness, embrace your confidence in your own personal style, and even learn to merge the two. Now let me make sure to clarify some things, I personally struggle with depression and anxiety, so I know these things to work, at least for me, with these two mental issues particularly.

I know you're asking, what makes you expert enough to write a book about this? Well, first things first you'd be surprised to find out that me writing a book makes me an expert, not the other way around. But beyond that, this book is all derived from my own personal life experiences and revelations paired with what I've learned. Oh yeah, I'm also a grad student getting a MAS in Clinical Mental Health Counseling, so I'm in a unique position to share from personal and professional (in training) standpoints.

So let's address a few things before we dive into this thing, shall we?

If you desire to, there is going to be at least one thing you can take from this book and apply to your life. Will everything work for you? Absolutely not, well I mean maybe cause they all work for me. But whether an actual tips works or it contributes to a shift in your perspective, it's all a win for me if it helps you to feel confident and take your mental health serious.

Will I make money from you reading this book, well yeah friend of course. But that's not what I'm doing it for. I want to make sure I share any and everything I can about my story and what I've learned to help you love yourself, embrace your style, and enjoy all the aspects of life there are to enjoy. Plus, I like talking to y'all anyway.

So, throughout this book you'll get a bit of my personal experiences, a little background from the counseling world, and maybe a few scriptures here and there because, you know, God. The same way I make sure to caveat things on my page, I love Jesus, but I'm not writing a Christian book. I'm writing a book and I just so happen to be a Christian, so there may be some Christian things in it because it's a part of who I am. That being said, if it's not for you, that's okay. Read this book with an open mind to grab on to whatever jumps off the pages at you. I'm still learning, and again, a lot of these things will be opinions that I have adopted because they work wonders for me, so I'm sharing.

If it doesn't apply to you, that's okay, read it anyway so you might be able to share it with someone else who needs to hear it. Not all of us will have the same mechanisms, but if we at least know the ones that others have, we can become more open and well rounded in our search for what works for us. Trying something to find out it doesn't work for you is better than not trying anything at all, because that definitely won't work for you.

If you picked up the book because you have a desire to better your style, you'll get that. If you picked up the book to better your mental health, you'll get that. If you picked up the book because we're besties, but not really, so you just wanna know me a little better, you'll get that too. It's all here in one aspect or another.

So, let's dive into the tea I'm about to spill, shall we?

It's A Mental Battlefield

Let's make sure, together, we have this understanding: Whether you lookin' to jazz up your style choices or needing a little help coping with your own mental health struggles, it all starts in your mind.

Sometimes people who don't understand mental health issues may think that it is a choice. "Just be happy." "You don't have anything to worry about, nothing is going to happen." "Pray about it." But the thing is, nobody makes the choice to HAVE depression. Nobody woke up and thought, oh yeah I think I'll take up anxiety today. Nah, that's not what it is. They are struggles of the mind. Now, I've said multiple times on my social media accounts that me personally, I know God has allowed me to continue to have anxiety and depression to do things like this, helping others knowing firsthand the experience, as well as it being utilized as a thorn. If you've read a bit of your bible, you know the thorn I'm talking about, my mental health issues continue to ensure that I never forget God, that I know there's nothing I can do in my own strength. To make sure I am capable of truly appreciating happiness and peace.

This is not to say, in any way shape or form, that God can't take it away if He wanted to. He absolutely can. But that's not my story. My mental health journey is a through one, not a delivered one. And that's okay. While that's the case, if you are believing God to free you from yours, I'm praying with you, because I believe it can happen. But I'm also praying that IF God decides He has a better purpose for you WITH those issues, that you are mature enough to accept that too.

Now, what in the world does that have to do with what this chapter title is? Everything. While we can't help if we have depression or anxiety, we can, to an extent, help how well we cope with it. Now, as you'll learn later, everyday won't be the same. You won't always come out on top, being the high functioning depressed you normally are, and that's okay. But what I do need you to understand is that your mind is where you have to go to war.

No matter what you desire to do with your body, for your body, or around your body, if you can't get the mind aspect of your being figured out and under control, you won't be able to fully reach the potential you have. This is easier said than done, trust me I understand. But the first thing we have to address is making sure you take hold of your own mind, to the best of your ability.

Have you ever heard the mind is a terrible thing to waste? What about your mind being powerful? Both of these things are completely accurate, at least as far as I'm concerned. But how? If you can figure out how to conquer something in your thoughts, you have now tapped into the power to conquer them outside of your mind.

Let me give you some examples. Let's say your mind thinks, "I really want some fries and a milkshake." At this point you have a couple of decisions, but let's keep it simple. If you continue to think about fries and a milkshake, how amazing they would taste together, the salt paired with the creamy ice cream, all that; eventually you are going to get fries and a milkshake right? Might not be the same day, but that thought will stay until it's satisfied, whether you realize it or not. Now let's say instead of dwelling on how amazing the fries and shake are going to be together you instead start thinking about how you are trying to save money, how you weren't happy the last time you looked at your body in the mirror, how you just bought apples and bananas. The more you think about the goals you may have that don't align with getting fries and a shake, the easier it becomes to exhibit self control and skip the fries and shake. Make sense?

Great! Now, that was a simple example, but the process is the exact same with everything that runs through your mind. Let's take it through another layer. Let's say your significant other or your friend does something to frustrate you. In that moment, you start thinking of all the petty, mean, aggressive things you want to say. Anger or hurt starts to flood your body so now you're thinking the worst possible things regarding how to respond, how to feel, and even assumptions about everything leading up to that situation. Here again, you have some choices. Does it feel better to lean into all of those dark thoughts and just let your mind run rampant?

Absolutely. So you could do that, OR you could acknowledge that your mind is starting to spiral and you can make yourself think more calming peaceful thoughts.

I did say it's easier said than done right?

Yeah, because the reality is it in fact DOES feel so much better to embrace all of those ridiculous thoughts and just let the emotion run it's course. That's cool if you're mature enough to keep your thoughts thoughts and not use them as a catalyst to do things that don't contribute to your growth. I, for one, have not reached that level of maturity because I'm liable to get real petty and start saying some of any and everything.

We don't want that.

The process of identifying what's happening in your mind at any given moment and making decisions on how to go about addressing those thoughts is what I'm talking about. For those who still need a little more, let me make it a bit more personal for you.

I have had all of my wisdom teeth removed. For those who don't know, they put you to sleep to take out your wisdom teeth, at least they did for me. Prior to the fella putting in the IV that sent the good stuff into my veins, they gave me a bit of laughing gas to go ahead and relax me. Well, I have an incredibly high tolerance, for everything. About five or so minutes go by, and this laughing gas has done nothing for me. The oral surgeon tells the dental assistant to go ahead and turn it up. Another few minutes and nothing. She basically had to turn it to the max for anything to start touching me.

During that process, I basically got too high too quick, so my mind started to trip a little. I'm still awake, and I can feel the oral surgeon searching for a vein, stabbing me multiple times trying to get the IV in. (Thank God I didn't feel any pain). While they're doing what they need to do to get me under to get them wisdom teeth out, my mind starts to freak out. My skin felt like little needles were pricking every inch of me, and all I could think was that I was going to die and I couldn't move.

One of two things could happen. I could have tried my best to start screaming and flailing around like a fish out of water, probably getting myself sent to the hospital, or I could remember that everything was fine and calm myself down mentally. I chose the latter. Was it trippy? You bet. Real out of body experience honestly, but I had to make the choice in my mind not to give in to the intruding thoughts that wanted to cause certain actions and reactions.

The same thing happened on my first plane ride, but that's a story for another day.

The point is, you have to make the decision, right now if you hadn't already, that you will remember the battle is in your mind and you have an advantage already knowing that. So how can you start conquering the battle in your mind?

Know Your Goals

What type of life do you desire to live? I'm not talking about a four-bedroom three-bathroom house on the hills, though that's great to know as well. But as a person, who is it that you desire to be? When you think about how you deal with your anger, ideally what does that look like for you? When you think about getting into a tussle with your friends and loved ones, what is the ideal response for you? When you consider how you want your appearance to look to others when you leave the house, what does that look like in your mind?

For me, my goals are to continue to grow in emotional intelligence and being mentally aware enough of myself that I can show compassion even when my emotions are high. I want to be able to keep in mind that everyone has their own struggle, so what I don't want is to resort back to my teenage way of dealing with things by insulting or offending someone because they've said or done something I don't like.

On a spiritual level, I want to make sure I can respond and react to things in whatever way is most pleasing to God.

These goals have become easier to embrace over time the more I've practiced. But in the process, it can be difficult. Feelings are fickle, they aren't always based on the reality of a situation but more so our perception of how things happened. Once I started to realize this, it became easier to begin to be more emotionally aware and allow my thoughts be the determining factor in decisions rather than my emotions.

Why would something like this be important? You remember the example I gave with the fry and shake? The second option required thoughts of goals. A goal is something you work hard towards. Without the goal of saving money or losing weight, what was the benefit of not having the fries and shake? There wasn't any. Having goals is going to be the determining factor in learning to control how you maneuver around your own mind because without them, there isn't much reward to choosing certain thoughts or actions.

Choosing not to murder someone is only rewarding because I have a goal of not just living as righteous of a life as I can live, but also I have a goal of sticking to my morals. If I did not have a moral standard or a relationship with God, would there really be a benefit in choosing not to pull the trigger if the right opportunity was presented?

Practice Self-Reflection

Knowing your goals is just the tip of the iceberg. In the times we live in, whether on social media or in real life, whether in or outside of the church, I'm sure we have all heard the word: Accountability.

Self-reflection isn't something that just sounds nice to do but it's an action that can help you hold yourself accountable. Let's be real. When other people hold us accountable, we tend not to like it very much. Especially if we haven't reached an adequate level of maturity to see past the embarrassment that comes with accountability. The thing about self-reflection, accountability to self, there is less embarrassment because we are the ones calling ourselves out. We have the opportunity to think all aspects through from the comfort of our own mind, often times without the help of anyone else.

How does self-reflection help this mental battle? It brings to the forefront accountability to those goals we just talked about. It also helps you to run down the situations you experienced, the thoughts you had, and what happened mentally as different thoughts occurred.

This process can happen situation by situation, day by day, week by week, or however floats your boat really. But from my experience, I have found the quicker I reflect on something, the easier it is to point out ways I could have handled something differently. It helps to remember the goals you've set and access what happened in your mind, and then outside of your mind as a result, and how that lines up with your goals. It's also a great way to learn how to lean into mental awareness.

Mental Awareness

When I say mental awareness, that's exactly what I mean: Being aware of your mental state at all times. When you are diagnosed with different things, not just mental illness, your doctor may tell you to know your triggers. For instance, I have eczema. I have to know what will trigger an eczema flare up to prevent it from happening. My skin is terrible really, so I also have to be mindful of what triggers outbreaks etc. Knowing those triggers helps me to prevent the things I can prevent.

Similarly, I have to know what triggers depression or severe anxiety episodes. This isn't always as simple as knowing the triggers that cause something physical, but it can help me try my best to prevent or control certain things. Another example? Sure! When me and my boyfriend first got together, I was still pretty young and my maturity level was used to a high school mentality. I quickly learned that social media was a trigger for my own insecurities that I took out on him. (Side note: It's no one else's responsibility to cater to your insecurities. If they love you, they'll try the best they can to help you through, but it's not their job to be less of themselves because you haven't dealt with insecurities that they didn't cause.)

Okay, rant's over, but anyway. Because I eventually recognized that, I personally deleted all my social media accounts. Now, that was a factor, but at that time social media wasn't helping my mental health struggle so I got rid of it. Fast forward three or so years, I had to get on social media again when I decided to publish my first book in 2020. (Isn't it interesting I went from leaving social media altogether to now having thousands of people watching me? Still kinda gives me the heebie-jeebies so I just don't think about that magnitude often.) The point I'm trying to make is, even after years went by and I dealt with insecurities, we still choose not to be friends or follow one another on social media today. We don't post one another or anything like that. It keeps our relationship ours alone, and it leaves no room for my mind (or the enemy) to play on old insecurities to start issues.

Being mentally aware is in part knowing your triggers but also knowing where you are mentally at any given time. What types of thoughts are you having? Why are those thoughts there? What's preventing you from thinking better? If you walked into your mind right now, what would be going on?

See being mentally aware is like cleaning up. If you pick up often you won't have to spend hours at a time trying to clean up the entire house. Take the time to inventory your mind. Not just the living room and kitchen though. Don't just become aware of the areas of your mind that are easy or that other people can see. It's the bedrooms, the closets, the cabinets of your mind that you need to make sure you pay extra attention to. Taking the time to clean those areas, becoming aware of what's housed there and how you can either fix it or learn to make it work for you, that's how you begin to start winning your mental battle.

Reading these things is easy to do. Practicing them is difficult. I'm a semi-pro now because I've been practicing for the better part of six years. But it didn't come overnight. It's difficult. Some of the things required of you can feel borderline unnatural, but if you stick to it, you're already more than halfway there. But, I want you to seriously consider these things and commit to seeing how well it works for you.

Now, I've already said this once, but you'll see it multiple times throughout the book: Not EVERYTHING that worked for me is going to work for you. But it's a starting place. Starting in your mind is a non negotiable. No matter how good you get at thrifting or looking well put together on the outside, eventually your mind can take over if you don't try to check and address it as often as possible. Start with taking inventory of your mind now, your thoughts, triggers, reactions, even your emotions. Knowing even a little of this will set your mind up to be open to understanding how some of these other tips can be used to help you, or how you can twist it to work in your favor.

Know What's In The Mirror (And What You Want To See)

I posed the question on my TikTok not long ago: When was the last time you looked in the mirror? It wasn't until I was grown when I truly started looking at myself in the mirror. I know that sounds crazy, so let me explain. Did I avoid mirrors altogether? Absolutely not, but I never actually took the time to look at me. See what I was doing was looking at how my clothes fit, making sure I didn't have anything in my nose or teeth. Stuff like that to make sure I looked my best when I left the house. But actually taking the time to SEE MYSELF, nah that wasn't something I started to do until recently.

It's important to know what's in the mirror. When we look at ourselves, what is looking back. This has many different aspects, and depending on where you are in life, you may only require one or two at a time, but all will be pertinent at one point or another.

Now, I'm not gone hold you; I was gung-ho about writing this book, I'm talking about knocking the word count out, excited about gettin' all this tea to you, then I hit this chapter. I realized this chapter is deep even though it's pretty simple. I got stuck, But it's cool, I took a lil trippy trip to the mountains, got some clarity, enjoyed some peace, and BAM: Here we are.

For most of my adult years, I have been very self-aware. I thrive on knowing what emotion I'm feeling, where I am in comparison to where I want to be, even when thought processes shift and change. I have come to enjoy the growth that comes with life rather than trying to rush to this or that like I used to. That all being said, when I started to take my mental health more seriously, I realized that I never looked in the mirror. Don't get me wrong; I looked in the mirror every day, brushing my teeth, washing my face, making sure my outfit was what I wanted it to be. But that was it. I wasn't looking at me; I was just looking at me.

Let me make it make sense. I wasn't taking the time to appreciate myself in the mirror. Physically, I wasn't actually taking a look at myself. I honestly didn't really know what I looked like. Beyond that, I wasn't taking the time to see all the aspects of me there were to look at, and what was looking back.

Now, when we talk about this mirror, I'm speaking literally as well as metaphorically. Literally, I do mean I now look at myself in the mirror. Obviously this is going to give me the most accurate physical representation of myself there is (as long as I am not in denial about what is actually looking back). Metaphorically, however, I had to learn to look at my life through the lens of God, and see me how He saw me. I started to pay attention to the things that couldn't be seen on the outside. I started to take inventory of my life. Where I was financially, emotionally, relationally, career wise.

Can I be honest with you? I realized I couldn't find any area of my life I was happy in. Generally anyway. I got to the point where everything was so depressing. And I stayed there for months, taking my own disappointment and pain out on those around me. I can't tell you the day, time, or hour a shift took place. I'm just not one that's great with my mind like that. But something happened. I went through old pictures and remembered how well I dressed, so I started having fun with my outfits again. I made the decision to put effort into my appearance, even when I didn't feel like it. I made the decision to make an effort every time I left the house, as opposed to only half way making an effort when I had somewhere of decent importance to go.

That one decision changed a plethora of things for me over time.

I know you're probably saying, Pearl Mae, you went off on a tangent there, what does this have to do with looking in the mirror? My answer: EVERYTHING.

If I didn't take the time to look in both the physical and metaphorical mirror, I wouldn't have been able to take inventory. I wouldn't have been able to know where I was in compared to where I wanted to be OR compared to where I used to be. This is where it's important to look in the mirror and see what's there, as well as what's not. And yes, both are very important. So let me break them both down so you're clear on the difference and how they are relevant to you.

What's In The Mirror

In other words, what do you see? Knowing what's in the mirror is simply, yet complexly, taking inventory of your life. Now, let me go ahead and let you know now: This can be a difficult process. The reality is, we don't like to "sweep around our own front door" as the old folks used to say sometimes. Because truth be told, our porches and patios can get a little dusty and a lot crowded from time to time.

Here, you need to establish where you are. What do the different areas of your life look like? You really get the opportunity to see what areas of your life you may really enjoy, areas that may need work, ones that are thriving, and ones that are dying. This can be hard to look at sometimes, but why?

We all want to be our best selves. Often times, we can portray to the world a version of ourselves that isn't completely accurate or whole. In doing that, it can become very easy to constantly live in this space where we forget what our life is actually like because we keep up the façade on our social media accounts or around our friends. We don't share with many, if any, the disappointing, shameful, painful, or even scary areas of our lives. Don't worry, I'm not here to tell you how important it is to share those things with others, though I will say the ones that love you can't help you unless you speak up. Instead, I'm here to help you deal with YOU.

No matter how many accountability partners we have, ministries we are a part of, courses we take, gym memberships we hold, or whatever else it is we try to use to hold us accountable; if we don't hold ourselves accountable, it just won't work. Sure, having that extra person or thing there is great, but it's there for extra help. You still have to make the decision on your own that you want something bad enough to learn to discipline yourself.

What does this have to do with knowing what's in the mirror? Well, seeing those things tend to bring a reality shock. Getting to the nitty gritty of where you are in various areas of your life give you an idea of what's what. You have to know the what's what to know the how's how, who's who, and the when's when.

Before we get into the next section, I want to make it abundantly clear that this may be a process for you. It may take a minute to deal with things, understand things, come to terms with things. And that's okay friend! Please understand that just because you may read this book in a matter of hours, days, months, etc.; it won't all happen as quickly as you read. I'm sharing things that have been YEARS in the making for me. It may be overwhelming, and that's okay. Make the decision to enjoy the ride, good and bad, and know that it's for the purpose of ultimately making your life better.

What Do You Want To See?

Now that you've gotten a chance to take a look in the mirror, what is it that you actually want to see? Whether you choose to evaluate this as you are taking that life inventory or after in two separate steps is completely up to you. Whatever works for you, works. Personally, I have found that knowing what I want to see first helps make what I currently see less overwhelming, but to each their own.

What's important is you know what it is that you want. There is no reason to get completely overwhelmed by where you currently are if you have no desire to be somewhere better. Meaning, you HAVE to know what you want to see when you look in the mirror. You have to know what you want to see when you evaluate your mental and spiritual health. You have to know what you want your financial situation to look like. And don't get me wrong, I am all for having the largest dreams imaginable, but you also have to put in some kind of effort to move in the direction of your ideal self.

Let's take a moment to evaluate this through example, shall we? Let's say I look in the mirror and I see a larger mid section than I used to. Okay, well am I okay with that mid section? If not, what is it that I want to see? Let's say I decide that I'd like my mid section to stick out a little less, and be a little more proportioned to my hips and thighs. Bet.

So now I know what I currently see, and I have an idea of what I want to see. With those two pieces of information, I can now make decisions, plan, to get from what to see, to what I want to see. Does that make sense?

Another example? Bet. So I look in the mirror of my finances and I see debt and not enough income to keep up. It's overwhelming for a moment, even depressing. It doesn't look like there is a way out. So after I get through the depressive aspects of the reality, what do I want to see? I want to see millionaire status. I want to see debt free, multiple streams of income, and abundance that can overflow to help others. I see where I am and I know where I want to be, now I can make steps to move toward what I want to see rather than stay stuck where I already am.

Please understand, that if done right, you may very well experience extremely overwhelming feelings in some areas of your life. Why? Well friend, some areas may be so far off from where you want to be that it seems impossible. The key word here: SEEMS. Plenty of things have seemed impossible until people found ways to accomplish them. I'm giving you the warning up front though, that overwhelming disappointment and feelings like you can't do it are going to come: Keep going anyway!

What's the worst that can happen?

That all being said, I want to try to give as much applicable and practical info as I can, so here are just a few things to do once you've taken that look in the mirror. Again, these are just a few things that can be done; you will have to find whatever is going to work for you. Use this as the launching pad to your journey.

One Area At A Time

If you are anything at all like me friend, you don't like when things are collectively in disarray. I won't necessarily say I want it all perfect, however as a person I desire to be the best version of myself I can ever be. That being said, if multiple areas of my life are out of wack, or I see many areas of my life need improvement, I would always try to fix it all at once. I had to learn that won't work.

When I bought my house, my boyfriend was rather frustrated with me. I had my apartment for another two weeks after closing on my house. He wanted to take his time with moving everything. Me, on the other hand, wanted everything moved on the day of closing. Not only did I want it all moved in, I proceeded to unpack and organize everything I possibly could because I couldn't function in what, to me, was chaos. Even after completely moving, I couldn't do the whole decorate one room at a time thing. Oh nah, not me. As soon as I knew what I wanted everything to look like, I had to decorate it all. I couldn't stand being in half completed spaces.

Because of this, you could imagine how extraordinarily overwhelmed I was when I looked around and couldn't find one area of my life I felt like I was doing well in. There were aspects of my personality I wanted to change. There was so much improvement that I felt needed to happen, and I didn't know how to do it all at once. To the point of reverting back to suicidal thoughts for a moment.

(Let's insert a side note here: Friend, it's okay to admit the dark places your mind goes to sometimes. Just make sure you can admit them in the safest places among people who know how to take it. I don't mind telling you that I've struggled with suicidal thoughts because for one, I know my thoughts are just that, thoughts. I don't intend to complete suicide. Also, I want you to know that you're not alone if you think or feel that way. Friend, life gets rough rough for some of us! It's cool, just keep swimming.)

First I came to terms with who I was. That was rough for me because my personality can be a bit, uh, harsh. I don't deal well in the areas of sympathy and empathy. I wish I did, but when I came to terms with the fact that I am not, it became easier to start figuring out how I could potentially elicit empathy, and when I would even want to. That all being said, you have to deal with one thing at a time.

I can't tell you what is going to be the most important thing for you to deal with. Your priorities may not look like mine, and that's cool. I need you to know that so in the event you get to lookin' at someone else's life you understand that your priorities will be very different from theirs. That's okay. Pick an area, maybe two and decide how you can move those areas in the right direction.

What I have found amazing about this is that once I start focusing on one area, I tend to see improvement in others as a result. It's not true for every area, but there is much overlap in ways that you can't always see until you start working it.

Set Goals, and MAYBE Timelines

Goals are always important to have. In the counseling world, goals help therapists to create some sort of measurement system in order to determine successful outcomes. You may be thinking that looking in the mirror and deciding what you want to see is, in itself, setting a goal; and you are most certainly accurate, but let's take it a step further. Looking at the big goal (i.e. what you want something to look like) can be overwhelming. We want to minimize being overwhelmed in an effort to ensure we are making progress. While I may be a pro in many areas of things now, I wasn't always that way. So what is easy for me to do now, I have to remember when it was difficult so I can help you! We tend to forget stuff like that sometimes, don't we? Aaaaanywho.

Here, I'm more so talkin' about setting mini goals. Smaller things that can motivate you and get you started in putting one foot in front of another so that you move toward that bigger goal. But Pearly Pearl, why you say maybe timelines? The simple answer: Anxiety. But lemme elaborate.

I had timelines for my life. Start having kids by 25, be done by 30. Be a millionaire by 30. Be debt free by this age. The list goes on and on and on. At 27, soon to be 28, I finally realized that having those timelines started to weigh on me in a way that I felt like they could never be accomplished if I passed the targeted age, or timeline. That being said, it's great to have timelines, I do still encourage them to help keep you on the right track, I just also firmly believe that you have to give yourself wiggle room. Timelines shouldn't be the strictest thing about your journey because that could leave you even more overwhelmed and even discouraged.

Essentially, set the goals, both big and small, but give yourself a little wiggle room for human error and life.

Be Consistent

Consistency is going to be a major factor in everything we talk about in this book. It doesn't matter how well something works for you if you decide to stop doing it. You also don't want to stop doing something after a pair of seconds because you aren't seeing results. Things take time. Whether you are moving towards the body you desire, the style you are going for, the mental awareness you need, no matter what it is you have to remember that it took years for you to get to this place. You didn't come out the womb in debt. It will take a minute for you to get to where you want to be; there aren't many overnight successes.

Let's put it in perspective. When you go to the doctor and they put you on a new medication, they typically want you to take that medicine for about 90 days before switching. During that time, they are able to see what it is or is not doing for you, your body, your symptoms, etc. They don't want you to just take the medicine for a week and then stop, they don't know if that medication could have worked or why it wouldn't work.

You have to take the same approach when trying things that have the potential to lead you closer to your destiny. I'm not saying you need to do something for years, but you do want to give it enough time to know for sure that it's not going to work for you. You also want to give it enough time to ensure that you get in the habit of doing it if it is for you. Keeping the image of what you want to see at the forefront of your mind can motive your consistency.

Be Real

It is imperative that you are real with yourself. You have got to be real about where you are, where you tryna be, and what it's gone take for you to get there. You can't really fake it till you make it with this thing. You want to be as strategic as possible and that can only be done if you're real about what's what. Don't be afraid to ask for help if you need it. Don't be afraid to stay up an hour later and do that research. You are going to have to be honest with yourself, even if you don't know how to be honest with others at the moment.

Are there other things you can do when you realize what's in the mirror and what you want to be in the mirror? Yeah, probably. But I can't run down the list of every possible action. This is a good starting point. It's enough to get the ball rollin as the old folks say. Now that we've gotten these first two chapters out of the way, we can get into the fun stuff: Style.

Understand,
Style is Subjective

Okay, let's get into this thing. If you bought this book because you're one of my TikTok friends, you already know me. But for the sake of those who may buy the book and THEN follow my TikTok (@PearlMae_), just know my style is my style.

So here's what we're going to do in this chapter. Let me set this chapter up for you, I kinda just bombarded you in the last two but we will be a little more chill. So first, we are goin' to talk about how I dress and how I got here, and then we will talk about how you can build confidence in the style or aesthetic you desire. Cool? Cool!

First things first: Fashion and style are two different things in my personal opinion. To me, fashion is the clothes, style is what you do with the clothes. When I think of fashion, I think high fashion, New York, just front cover of a magazine. Style, on the other hand, I think about regular folks and how they put things together. It can change over time, it's different for every person, and most importantly: It's subjective.

Let's talk about my style. It's unique to say the least. I thoroughly enjoy putting together the most unforeseen items and looking dang good in it. But beyond looking good, I mentally enjoy the process of putting something together that many others wouldn't think of and then getting compliments. Now, I don't really have one specific aesthetic, I pretty much wear what I want to wear when I want to wear it and the only thing consistent about it is that I mix prints and patterns more often than not.

You'll see what I mean on my page but basically all of my outfits are out of the box and not everyone's cup of tea. And that's okay! (Cause I still look dern good regardless).

It took me a while to be able to be as confident as I am in my style choices, and be in a position to be completely unbothered when someone doesn't appreciate my creative style. First, I had to get out of the headspace that I had to please, or look like, the people around me. For the longest time I was looking at other people and taking on their style choices as what I was supposed to look like, whether it was in school, church, or a professional setting. Once I realized that mentally I was getting dressed with the idea of being accepted by others in mind, I could unpack that and determine that I wanted to get dressed FOR ME. After that, I had to accept that getting dressed for me meant I couldn't allow myself to determine how good my outfit was based on how many comments I got on it. I had to make sure that every time I walked out of the house, especially in what some would consider to be risk-taking outfits, I would be okay if not one person complimented me on it. Once I got those two things down, I realized that there were so many other people who had the desire to be more bold in their outfit choices, and would compliment me on my confidence. Que starting a TikTok to encourage women in this very area.

So, we got a little bit about me out of the way, but don't worry I'll be going into more details a little later to help you out.

I've asked time and time again, so many people, what scares you about doing something different in your style? What's holding you back? Often times the answers range anywhere between not thinking they would look good, their weight, or just being afraid that people will say rude things to them. The reality is all of these things are in our head. So let me share how you can step out.

The very first thing you are going to need to understand is that style is subjective. Pearl Mae, you keep saying that, but what does that mean? That means there is no right or wrong answer to style. Just because someone else wouldn't wear something the way you do does not mean what you're wearing is wrong. This is something you are going to have to make sure you grab hold to so that you can effectively apply everything we are about to talk about. So, before we get into these tips, say it with me: Style is subjective. Style is what I make it. There is no right or wrong.

Got it? Bet. Let's go.

Get Dressed For You

I have another chapter dedicated entirely to this point, so we won't get into too tough but it's important enough to mention a time or few. Whether it be in your sense of style, your mental health, your career, your relationship, please understand it is ultimately for you. You only have your life, nobody else's. That being said, don't indulge in things that don't make you happy, that don't cater to the things that bring you joy. We tend to succumb to the idea that struggle is normal and necessary; life is hard, blah blah whoop whoop. Yes, these things are true for some. You may go through some rough seasons no doubt, but in the areas where you can make the choice on whether to tolerate something or not, whether to do something or not, choose the things that's going to bring you joy. Choose the things that's going to make you happy. When it comes to an outfit, baby wear it! Who are you hurting by the outfit you choose to wear? My bet would be nobody. If it makes you happy, if it makes you feel sexy, if it boosts your confidence, well sugafoot: Wear that thang.

It's Okay If Some People Disagree

As difficult as it can seem to understand in the moment, it's important to understand that it is perfectly okay if someone doesn't like your style. Throughout this book we've talked about it all being about you, and it is. That being said, it's important that we also take up the understanding that there will be people who may not be appealed by our sense of style, and that's okay. The same way that not everyone may have the same belief or viewpoint on a topic as you, they may not have the same viewpoint on your style. You may find that you don't like someone else's. And that's fine. Why is it fine? Because we understand when it comes to style, it's a lot like "beauty is in the eye of the beholder." Art lovers love different forms of art. Some may enjoy paintings over statues while others may enjoy poetry over music. As long as we all grab on to the understanding that the way we view beauty may be different, but it's all what we find beautiful to ourselves.

It will be beneficial to train your mind to truly accept that not everyone will see things your way. This will help you in the event that you do get discouraging remarks or opinions, but you'll be able to handle it because you've accepted that not everyone will look at things like you.

You're All The Reason You Need

There doesn't have to be any fancy vacation getaway or expensive dinner in order for you to wear things. No events or plans have to be made. Now if that's how you prefer to pick your outfits because that works for you then that's one thing, but generally, the only reason you need to wear something is because you want to. No matter where you're going, what the temperature is, or who will be there. There are so many unspoken "rules" when it comes to how we present ourselves for others to see, but we are breaking away from that structured thinking to allow our inner child to be free, rather than locked up behind societies rules.

Look On The Outside How You Want To Feel On The Inside

Strategic self-anticonformity. SSA for short. Now you may be thinking, "Uhhhhhh, what?" Let me help you out. SAA is what the psychology world now calls "reverse psychology." You know about that right? We use it somewhat loosely in everyday life, and there are plenty of people out there who use it as a manipulation tactic, but here let's see how it's positive benefits may be useful to us, shall we?

Reverse psychology is simply advocating for behaviors or actions that differ from an intended or desired outcome. You advocate for the opposite of what you really want in hopes of persuading your intended outcome. While this can have negative effects when being improperly practiced on other people, if done the right way with good intentions for ourselves, it could potentially shift not just desired outcomes, but also how we look at ourselves.

So here's how this is relevant. As you can see from the title, this chapter is focusing on looking on the outside how you want to feel on the inside. How can reverse psychology be applied to this?

I don't know about you, but let me first share what happens to me when I get depressed. Symptoms of a more severe depressive episode for me can vary from having no desire to leave the house, not getting out of bed, not showering for days, forgetting to eat, having little to no drive, and not interacting with loved ones. All of these things typically, at least used to, hinder me from properly taking care of myself and caring about my appearance during one of these episodes. Because of this simple fact, I went years forgetting that I even enjoyed putting unique outfits together in the first place. That along with the fact that I had started getting dressed for the approval of others hindered my style growth for years. But I'm sure I'll get into that later.

Taking that into consideration, the trick is to do the opposite of what we feel like in hopes of manipulating the mind to feel how we desire to feel. So it looks something like this. Let's say I have something to attend, something I have to participate in, but I don't feel excited, happy, attractive, social. Despite how I feel, or what I'm actually thinking, I'm going to dress to impress. I'm going to put on the best outfit I can at the time, do my hair and makeup, whatever I would do if I was genuinely at my best.

Without all those words, let me put it to you how my grandmother would: "Fake it till you make it."

While generally speaking I don't like that phrase, especially depending on how people are using it, in this instance it's exactly what we are doing. I'm not saying this would be an everyday thing, though sometimes it may be. But giving it a try even one out of every three or four bad days could make a great impact on the mental affects it may have.

One day, I had the bright idea (or maybe remembered someone saying it somewhere, who knows!) that I would make the effort one time a week, no matter how I felt, no matter what the weather was, and no matter who was going to be around. Sunday. Sunday was the day I started with. I went through my photos (thank God for technology that can keep our pictures forever) and remembered the different outfits I used to wear to church.

Scrolling and scrolling, up and down and up and down again. I couldn't quite pinpoint where, but I realized I started doing the bare minimum when going to church.

That wasn't like me. So seeing that, remembering what it used to feel like, I made the decision that no matter how I felt on Sunday, albeit I wasn't sick, I would get up and put together the best outfit I could and go to church. Guess what happened? Not only did I remember, but I could feel what it was like to be me again. I could feel the appreciation of the art of my own style. I started to have the desire again to dress for myself rather than the people around me. I could even breathe in the familiar scent of my eclectic, sometimes busily unique style. I was starting to feel confident about who I was again.

Before I knew it, I went from just Sunday's to getting dressed more often, even if just doing mundane things. All that from making the decision a few times a month to look much better than I actually felt.

The thing is, in the same manner what we do on the inside affects our bodies on the outside, what we do on the outside has the potential to affect what we do on the inside. Feeling the freshness of your body after a hot shower could make the difference in you staying in bed in a dark room all day or going outside for a breath of fresh air. Doing something different to your appearance, putting on a nice outfit, doing your makeup, scalping a new lace front, these things can contribute to you enjoying yourself for a moment. The more your look in the mirror and see pieces of yourself that bring you joy, the more your mind can cling to joy and peace rather than the depression and anxiety that may have a grip on it at the moment.

Something similar to this is my thought process when getting dressed for the gym. I personally only go to the gym about 4-6 months out of the year. While I'm sure this will change as I get older, but that's pretty much all it takes to maintain the body I enjoy. Knowing this, every time I know its time to get back in the gym, I wear things that motivate me. Here's what I mean. At this point, I have an idea of the body, or figure, I feel best in. Knowing this, I'll wear clothing items or combinations that help me envision what I want my body to look.

Let me make it plainer. My preference is a slimmer stomach, wider hips, defined shoulders/arms, and large hamstrings/quads. With this in mind, I made sure to pick out pants or shorts that were high wasted, made my butt look nice, and a shirt that would either make me feel small in it or complimenting the figure I was going for. Creating these illusions work for me because gym mirrors are everywhere (if y'know, y'know). Getting a glimpse at the figure I already had but in the light of how I wanted it to look motivated me to do the last rep or do another set.

If you haven't caught a theme yet, I enjoy looking at myself in the mirror. Not in a weird, obsessed type way though. I realized that I had been looking in the mirror without actually looking at myself for years. I honestly didn't even know what I looked like. Because of that, I make it a point to not just look at the mirror but to actually look at myself in the mirror every chance I got. Some days are still a struggle, I'll find it difficult to actually look at myself because I don't feel like being accountable to myself in that moment, and that's okay. I just can't let that be the case everyday, or even every time I look in the mirror.

This chapter is pretty self explanatory I think, but let me make sure I make a few tangible things clear so you can see if any of these things may help you. Don't forget, just because something doesn't work for you doesn't mean nothing will work. Every person is different, the way you deal with mental illness will be different as well.

Get Dressed at Least Once A Week

Sometimes all you can do is make an effort once. Pick a day of the week. Pick that day to be a day that you get dressed to some capacity or another, every week. It won't matter if you're depressed, anxious, have anything to do or not. That day you'll put the effort towards your outfits. Make it a self care day if you need to. That day is a day dedicated to you spending time with yourself, no matter what.

Create a Routine

The same way that you picking a day to get dressed is a routine, you may need to create more frequent routines. I've recently taken up a skincare routine. Where I used to just wash my face with soap and water in the morning and spot treat as needed, I started putting more effort into that routine. I found that doing that one thing everyday, whether I did anything else or not, made me feel a little better. Even if it didn't make me feel better in the moment, the idea that the way I'm taking care of my face now will create great results later makes me feel accomplished.

Here, creating a skincare routine benefits the way my skin looks not only now, but later as well. You're routine may be going to the gym, stretching regularly, anything that can contribute to doing something outwardly that has the potential to shift what's going on on the inside over time.

It may not work everyday. Some days you may try, and it still doesn't work. It's okay friend. I recently posted a TikTok about an experience just like this. I was stuck in the house on a quarantine and I thought to myself, "I'll play dress up, I still have those dresses I didn't take that photo shoot in."

Everything was going great, until it wasn't. I put on the first dress, tossed on my wig, and despite the fact I couldn't quite take the pictures I wanted to, it was a success. But when I got to the second dress, the dress I was most excited about, everything went wrong. The dress didn't fit anymore. I didn't like any of my wigs with it. I didn't like what I saw in the camera, and quickly tears formed. I had to unpack that in that moment. With tears in my face, I took my wig off, stopped trying to hold the dress together, and looked at myself in the camera until I found the beautiful things.

It took a while, and it was more uncomfy than I had prepared for, but I did it because that was an opportunity I had to grow.

It's For YOU,
NOT Sister Susan

The older I got, the more I started to learn about myself. I don't know about anyone else, but I had a lot of things about myself that I didn't know. Even more interesting, I found that I had many "beliefs" or ideas that I held not because they were my own, but because they were taught to me or were the societal norm.

2021 really was a year where I got to learn more about myself in ways that I hadn't had to before. I was pushed to my limits with stress, medical diagnoses and surgery scares, family health problems, and a rapidly changing work environment (not for the better either). All that being said, I had made the vow that 2021, my

27th year, I would dedicate it to allowing myself to be who I am. No matter what that looked like. I decided I was going to fully embrace everything about myself: The things I liked, the things I didn't like, the things that could and the things that couldn't be changed. It was the best thing I could have ever done.

Somewhere around April-ish of 2021, I started to get my groove back. At least as far as my style was concerned. I started looking back at pictures and realized between the panorama, depressed, and a genuine disinterest in putting effort in, I had let my style go. I couldn't remember the last time I was in an outfit I enjoyed wearing. One I was proud I had put together. So I started getting dressed again. While that seems simple enough said out loud, it ran much deeper. I started to evaluate what my motives were when I was getting dressed. In doing that, I found that much of what I was putting on, or how I was pairing things, I was doing based on what I thought other people would like. I wondered if the outfit would do well on Facebook, I thought about different people at church and what they may say about it, I thought about posts I had seen on social media about these kinds of clothes or those kind, I thought about what was vastly considered "appropriate and inappropriate" and why. Do we see a pattern here? A theme perhaps?

When I realized that the subconscious and even unconscious habits I had of thinking about how other people would feel or perceive me based on the things I chose to wear, I changed the game. But it wasn't over night. What I said? April-ish? Yeah, well I didn't have my complete, FORGET THIS I'M WEARING IT FOR ME moment until the end of May.

At the end of May, one of my homies got married. Now, I knew this homie would stand for me flaunting my shh. I got a bomb jumpsuit, got some new shoes, but would you believe I still found myself afraid of wearing what I wanted to wear? Why? Well, hold on, before I tell you that let me give you a picture of said jumpsuit. The legs were skinny and almost a legging type material, very form fitting. As for the top, it was a simple twist top, and by twist top I mean you twist it around your neck much like a bikini top and there's enough fabric to cover "most" of your boobs. Got the picture? Bet, okay now back to the answer.

I knew there would be a good amount of church folk at her wedding. The idea that the same people I worshipped with would see me, at a non church event, and talk about me because of what I chose to wear was the problem. While I did put a blazer on for the ceremony, which was at the church, the reception was fair game and I wasn't going in with that blazer on.

That event pushed me so far out of my comfort zone that I was propelled into myself. That's crazy right? But that's what happened. I walked around confidently in the outfit that made me feel amazing, and guess what happened? I had a great time! I did it. I made the decision to wear what I wanted, what made me feel good, and made up in my mind before leaving the house that I didn't really care what anyone had to say. Now, I'm not going to lie and say that I still didn't overcompensate just a little by giving a "warning" to some folks, but I can assure you I don't do that anymore.

Why did I tell you all of this? Because getting dressed is for you. It's not for your spouse, your children, your friends, the people on the internet, your pastor, prophet, pool boy, or party planner. Now, don't get me wrong, there will be times when you will probably get dressed for someone else, i.e. putting on something special for your spouse, but that's not the kind of thing we're talkin about right now.

At the end of the day, Sister Susan, the person (or people) in your mind that you're worried about when you're putting clothes on, they aren't there with you at night. They aren't looking at your body in the mirror with you. As a matter of fact, baby THEY NOT BUYIN YO CLOTHES! I don't care what your shape is, what your title is, what your body size is, none of that. You know what else I don't care about? I don't even care if I like what you decide to put together and wear. Why? Because you didn't get dressed for me, you got dressed for you.

In my opinion, it is so easy for us today to be overwhelmed with the opinions of others that may or may not be held by a large group of people and deemed the "standard" when in reality, it's just their opinion. A great example of this is the bearing social media can have on relationships. I can't tell you how many posts I would see daily about "if he/she don't post you red flag", or something along those lines. The overall consensus is that for a relationship to be valid, both parties must be constantly posting one another on their social media accounts. The gag with that is, we don't see what happens behind the scenes of these picture perfect "relationship goals."

In the same way, we don't know what type of problems, issues, or anything of the sort the next person may have, and we certainly can't tell from pictures. That being said, what's stopping you from wearing the type of clothes you want to wear? Whether you want to wear more revealing clothing, weather you want to get into being more eccentric, whether you are looking to adopt a street wear look, or all of the above, what is holding you back from truly enjoying what you put on your body on a daily basis?

I look back on pictures now and it's so clear to me that I could see when I was struggling with my outfits, when I was getting dressed for other people, and when I was actually getting dressed for me. There was a clear evolution. That evolution helped me not just put together dope outfits that I share with the world on social media, but it reconnected my in some areas and reintroduced me in others to myself. More specifically to my own subconscious.

Your subconscious is the area of your mind that you aren't fully aware of most of the time, but it has the potential and power to affect your feelings, emotions, and even your actions. Your subconscious is not completely in focus, more like working in the background. Your unconscious mind is an automatic process, a place where your memories and motivation are. While your unconscious isn't typically open for retrospection, your subconscious is a gateway to the automatic process. Why is this important? Because if you start to learn how to become aware of what's going on in your subconscious mind, you can in turn learn more about your unconscious mind. This knowledge gives you the power to either change things, if they can be changed, or have a better understanding so you can effectively maneuver and work at conquering things that may be a hindrance.

Depending on the type of therapy a person chooses to participate in, there are a number of therapeutic processes that look at bringing memories and motivations of the unconscious forward in efforts to help reach a desired goal.

So who says style can't be included in therapy? You remember when we talked about getting dressed to trick our minds into feeling better? Yeah, that's a therapy process, albeit not one necessarily used by all counselors today. The point is, when you start taking something as simple as the outfits your choose to wear and really evaluate yourself as you put outfits together or get dressed, you can build that self-confidence and so much more. So again I ask, what's holding you back?

So many women have told me they wished they could wear this or that, when I ask why they can't, the answers are typically the same. Either they are concerned with their weight or body figure, or they think they will not look right. So let's talk about that.

Starting with weight. Friend listen to me, while I'm not saying this is guaranteed to work for you, I'm just saying I noticed this did work for me. When I gained weight, I had to learn to love my body, no matter where it was. Sure I wanted to lose weight, sure I wanted to look the way I used to, but more than that, I wanted to learn to love myself no matter what part of the life process I was in. Now, obviously I could tell you what many others would probably tell you: Go work out, go on a diet, changing your lifestyle. Yeah, that's all cool and whatnot, and it is definitely accurate advice, but for me personally I've found that when I love myself more, I can actually enjoy the process of losing weight, or whatever else I may be doing at the time for that matter.

How did I learn to love my new body? Well, it was honestly accidental. We were getting ready to go to Vegas for vacation. I had been in the gym but not long enough to get a perfect bikini body. I started trying clothes on and realized that I had been trying to still fit in clothes that were bought for my old size. The first thing that made the biggest difference: Making sure I was wearing the right size! That may sound ridiculous to you, but hear me out. You don't gain weight overnight, it's a gradual process, So gradual in fact that you're going through everyday life and the next thing you know, those jeans are a little more snug than they used to be. That top fits a little tight around the arms. We always talk about not shopping until we lose weight etc. But what about your current body? It deserves to have nice things put on it, even if you're ashamed of where you are right now. I mean for some of us buying a gym membership doesn't motivate us the way we think it does, so why should we not get a new outfit just because we intend to lose weight?

Once I realized what my new size was, I started getting clothes that I felt accentuated my body. I don't wear the kinds of things now at 210lbs that I wore when I was still 150lbs. My stomach has gotten little more "plump", so I found all things high wasted to be of great comfort. I also stopped wearing form fitting dresses like that, and even changed the frequency and way I wear pencil skirts. I learned what items worked best for me to accentuate the features I appreciated and the ones I didn't want to draw much attention to.

That's it. Me deciding to buy clothes for where my body was at the time made me feel confident and reminded me that I was still beautiful. Appreciating my body despite it's imperfections not only motivated me to get in the gym and create the body I desired, but it brought out a confidence that I only got by loving myself.

Now, for all you girlies who were thinking, "Pearl, I WISH I was 210lbs. It's not that easy." Babe, listen, who said it was easy for me? We don't have to compare weight or struggles, because both experiences are valid. While being in the low 200's is as large as I have ever been, the concept is the same across the board. It doesn't matter what your weight is or what your figure looks like, you just have to make sure you're wearing what's your size and things that make you feel pretty right where you are. And again, let's not forget who you are getting dressed for: You. You're getting dressed to feel good about and for yourself. So all that has to matter is it looks good to you.

Y'all get the gist right? If not, add me on TikTok and comment your questions on a video so I can expound. (HA! You see that shameless plug there?) Okay, anywhos. On to the second answer I get all the time: I don't think it will look right on me. Listen, at this point I am convinced that everything in life is simply trial and error if you're truly wanting to live it out for yourself. Your style is no different. The people, who give me this answer, in my opinion, are typically looking at my outfit and picturing the exact same outfit on themselves. But what works for me won't work for everybody. That doesn't mean your style has to be plain Jane, unless that's the style you're going for. It just means you have to work at what you feel you like and what looks good for you.

My style has evolved over the years, and it's fluid. There are people who pretty much wear the same types of clothes all the time, but not me baby. One thing about it, and two things for sure: I'm gone switch that thang up! Because my mood changes, the looks I'm going for change based on a number of factors, and as we just read, my body changes. It took years for me to get to this place. The only consistent thing in my style would be that I enjoy mixing prints and patterns, or combining oddly unique things that others may not think to join together.

That being said, there are still plenty of things I see on other women that I think look amazing on them but I feel just wouldn't look right on me. Does that mean I stick to what I've always done? Absolutely not my friend. In those instances, I look past the pieces another person has on as they are and I get creative. I take inspiration from what they are wearing and I use that inspiration to create something that is fitting for me. I personally tend to see myself as an artist, clothes being my canvas to create something beautiful in the form of outfits.

Okay friend, so what have we learneedddd?

That's right, your style is unique to you and it doesn't matter if anyone else likes it or not. Now y'all know I'm not trying to give you these gems and not at least make an attempt to tell you how. What we've talked about so far is all about how you perceive things in your mind, but what actions can you take toward being confident enough to embrace your own style no matter what anyone else has to say?

Find Your Hype Man Friends

First off, if your friends aren't hyping you already, you may want to find new friends but that's a topic for another day. Let's be real, we all know what friends we can call on for what. All friends are not created equal in all circumstances. Me personally, I don't ask my friends their opinions on my outfits anymore, but that's because of the confidence I now have. But I did at one point. For instance, y'all remember that wedding I said I went to? I went through a number of different outfits, all some level of risqué, and guess who I texted to ask about them? THE BRIDE. Why? Because one thing about it, she gone hype you up when it comes to an outfit. Especially that kind of outfit. This worked for me for two reasons. One, it was her event so her approval was all I needed. Second, she was a hype man, she made me feel good about the outfit choices I had, and made me feel confident that I would look good in any of them. This confidence pushed me to wear the one I felt best in.

These friends may not always be the same ones, but you know your friends the same way they know you. The friend who is overly opinionated may not be the best friend to ask in this scenario, not because you don't love them but because you only need people who will hype it up for you if you really like it. Any criticism may be unmerited and harmful to the confidence you're trying to build in your style. And let's be honest, no criticism hurts like that of a friend. So strategically ask people what they think about an outfit, the ones who you know are going to hype you about it rather than look at you sideways. The "friends" I had who always hit me with the "I just don't want you out here looking a mess" or something similar to the "I'm looking out for you because I love you" spill, yeah that was a no go for me. Considering style is subjective, just because you think it looks "a mess" doesn't mean I do, so I won't give the opportunity for my subconscious to move based on how you're going to react. There's always a difference in making sure I don't have nothing in my teeth or my wig ain't crooked compared to your opinion on the actual outfit.

So for those friends, I never ask them about an outfit beforehand, I just show up with it on. (Side note: Just showing up with an outfit on, whether you're confident or not, looks confident. That gets compliments.)

Wear it in the House First

Do you think you can guess how many times I put on an outfit that doesn't do it for me initially, but I wear it anyway? It's more often than you think. Recently there were about two or three different items that I really wanted to wear, at the same time. So I figured out how to put them all together. The problem was the outfit on my body didn't quite click with the vision I had going in my head. When it just doesn't quite click, I let it grow on me. I get dressed in enough time that I have a few extra minutes to just look at myself in the mirror, walk around the house and then look at myself in the mirror again to let the outfit grow on me.

Sometimes we can be so quick to just take an outfit off when we just haven't given it the same opportunity we give some of these no good dust buckets that come across our lives. Did I type that out loud? Okay anyway, yeah.

One of the most empowering things you can do is something for yourself, by yourself. In the sanctity of your own home, or your own room, even your own bathroom if that's what it takes. Not having confidence to do something around others simply indicates you're not fully confident just doing it with yourself. Taking the time to put on an outfit that may be a little daring for you and wearing it around the house can show you how you may feel wearing things like that. It also helps boosts your ability to love yourself in that condition. You'll get comfortable with that version of you, the version that is happy and excited about the things you put on. When you're that happy, it's difficult for people to change that for you.

Why are kids so confident wearing their favorite princess costume to the grocery store with their light up shoes and a cape? Because they've already worn it around the house a million times and love the way they felt, strangers or the opinions of strangers don't faze them.

Just Wear It

I tell people all the time, the best way to get comfortable and confident in doing something is to just do it. I walk out of my house all the time in whatever it is that I want to wear. Whether I'm feeling it or not at the time doesn't matter, I'm building the habit. There seems to be a misconception that you'll get talked about or something like that, but let me clarify. Will people talk? Yes, absolutely. But in the real world, you know the non social media one we actually exist in, people don't say rude things about your outfit to your face. On the contrary though, what people WILL do, they will compliment you in the real world. There have been plenty of times I've worn something and people I don't know have complimented it, because they liked it. While I have confidence, something about someone else acknowledging that I look nice helps to boost it. You are far less likely to hear someone say something rude about your outfit than you are to hear someone say something positive. Those positive reactions will boost your confidence, encouraging you to keep doing it.

Post It

Now, this one is a little more on the advanced side. Posting things on social media can be hit or miss. I wouldn't encourage this to be the first thing you do if you're still trying to build your confidence in your style choice, unless you are posting to a friends only type account like a Facebook. Even then be careful. I don't want to be negative in this suggestion, I just want to be real and set expectations. Once something is on the internet, people oddly find a sense of entitlement to vomit their opinion all over your post. Of course some social media platforms are worse than others when it comes to this, which is why it's important to be aware of the people exposed to your content if you're still struggling a little.

That all being said, there is a great opportunity that many people will like it and further give compliments and encourage you. My TikTok community is amazing, and while I do have people who don't like all of my outfits all the time, it's okay. I am confident enough in myself and what I do, backed by the plethora of DM's and comments I get about how I inspire others that those negative comments don't get under my skin. That encouragement I get from the people who support me further enhances my confidence.

If you're feeling froggy, post that thing and see what happens. OR, you could always post and set the privacy settings to only yourself. What does that do? It gives you a place to see yourself on a social media platform the way others would, even if nobody else will actually see it. I know plenty of people who post on TikTok and keep it where they are the only ones who can see it. Almost like their own little video diary. This is always an option.

Okay, did we get all that? Good cause now, we are about to talk about the wardrobe, more specifically the budget for the wardrobe!

You Don't Have To Break The Bank

Just in case your heart dropped when I made all those suggestions about a new wardrobe, it's okay friend, I GOT YOU! I know that just because I shop a lot doesn't mean everybody can, does, or even has the desire to. Honestly, I feel like a number of people tend not to think they can change their style because they don't have the money. But what if I told you, you don't have to break the bank!

It's honestly not about how much money you have to spend on clothes, it's about what you do with the clothes you spend money on. Friend, please understand you DO NOT have to spend tens and hundreds of dollars on different items in order to look nice. It's really not about how expensive an item or outfit is. I've worn outfits that have cost hundreds of dollars, and I've worn outfits that cost less than $50.Guess what? I looked good in both!

So what I want to do is share a few different things that you can do to change up your style, embrace whatever style is personal and unique to you, and do it without spending a lot of money. Unless you cool with that, but even still, read the whole chapter anyway, it may still give you some tips.

Clean Out Your Closet

The very first thing you should do, is go through your closet. If you're anything like me, you have a hard time letting go of clothes you wore years ago, friend we not getting back to our high school size (at least I'm not). Let some of those clothes go. Now, before you roll your eyes at me, here me out. We aren't necessarily going get rid of everything, but you do need to go through your inventory and see what you're working with. I try to do this at least twice a year. But what are you looking for when you go through your closet?

First and foremost I'm not going to tell you to look for clothes you haven't worn in a certain amount of time. A lot of people will tell you that and if it works for you then great, but let me tell you why that part isn't important to me. I personally don't wear the same outfit more than once. And I go pretty far between wearing the same item again. That's just me. Because of that, I may only get one wear out of something in any given year, but I still intend to wear it again. Plus my style is so eclectic, I'm always looking for something I thought I'd never wear again because it fit the look I was going for.

What I will tell you to do though is first look for anything you feel doesn't fit the style you think you're consistently going for. For instance, I know that I'm not the girl who wears form fitting church dresses anymore. I have no use for them. Add to that that I'm not big on dresses anyway, and they are more there for comfort and convenience, that let's me know I don't need any of the ones in my closet. When you're going through your closet and find items that you need out of the way, you want to make two different piles: Clothes to throw away and clothes to give away.

When you're doing this, try to also get in the habit of thinking of at least two to three different looks you can create with each item. This will help you see the versatility in a garment as well as get your creative juices going and visualizing that style you're looking for more often.

With your two piles, one is of course self explanatory, just throw the clothes away. The second pile, however, has different options. The first option is if you're planning to give those items to a friend or family member, someone that you know personally. Second, you can decide to donate them to a local organization or charity. The last option, however, may help if you need a little extra cash to replace some of those items. You can sell them. When I started typing this, I was only focused on one selling method, but then I remembered we are now in the Lord's year 2022, and there are different options with this too. You may find a local shop that buys clothes in order to resell them. This option does have a few downfalls though in that the cost given for items isn't much and they may or may not accept the items based on their business needs at the time. Alternatively you can sell your clothes online yourself. There are many apps and mechanisms to selling online that could definitely generate more income for you.

Whatever you decide to do with the clothes, make sure you're going through that closet.

Shoes and accessories too. Yeah, I know friend, I know.

Thrift Shop

At the time of me writing this, I have a non profit Sain d'Esprit Directive Inc. One of the biggest things I plan to get off the ground in 2022 is our thrift store. Thrifting isn't for everyone, I'm not going to lie to you. But it can be an amazing process if you do learn and enjoy it. Thrift stores are going to be your cheapest option when it comes to revamping your wardrobe.

When going in the thrift store, one of the best pieces of advice I think I can give is think outside of the box. When looking at items, don't automatically let their original intent be how you look at it. Train your mind to think of an alternative method of wearing it first, then look at it's original purpose. But why? Because this ensures each item you're buying has enough versatility to add value to your closet, and you also end up with great pieces and outfits that you may not have considered just looking at an items original intent. For instance, let's say you walk into a thrift store. I always go to the men's section first. Looking at a men's shirt is your first thought a shirt, or a dress? See I'm looking at a men's shirt, and it's size, and I'm automatically thinking: Can this be cute as a shirt dress? What would I wear under it with the button's open? What pants would I wear if I wore it buttoned up? Can I tie it around my waist and it fall cute?

You see what I did there? In looking at one item, I thought about four different outfits I could use it for. Even if you don't come up with all the particulars right then and there, the question is still: How many ways can you use this shirt?

Of course there will be some things that you may or may not be able to think of alternatives, and that's okay. I don't want you to think I'm saying don't buy anything you can't think of alternatives for. If you like it, buy it. But do try to make sure you can get as many pieces as possible that can offer you a variety. This way, if or when there are times that money is tight, you can use the same garment multiple ways so it doesn't look like you are constantly wearing the same thing over and over.

Optimize Variety

What have I been saying this whole time? Variety, different options, multiple ways to wear something. Optimizing the ability to transform different items into things they weren't initially intended to be helps save money. To recap, seeing multiple ways to wear an item can keep you from feeling like you don't have anything to wear, or like you're wearing the same thing over and over.

Having multiple ideas also enhances your ability to embrace your style. It helps you see the different things you do and don't like without having to take clothes back or get rid of them because they didn't work. Looking at different ways to wear or style an item also helps with the longevity of your wardrobe. Think of it like period panties. Most of us didn't go buy brand new panties specifically for our periods. Nah, we bought new panties, and then when they got old they became our period panties. In the same way, constantly think about not just what an item can do for you but what it has the potential to do for you later as well. This helps you enjoy your wardrobe, no matter what stage it's in. It also helps when your weight fluctuates because what may not serve you in one capacity now can shift and serve you in another.

Budget

The reality is, you can live whatever life you feel you deserve, you may just have to work for it. That being said, if you don't want to thrift, and you want to be able to get other clothes that you want, budget for it. People would always talk about how I shop all the time or talk about me being rich because I shop often. The reality is, I enjoy shopping so I made sure it was a part of my budget. The same way people budget for bills, food, and entertainment, I budget for what I enjoy as well.

With that being said, you have to be realistic with where you are and where your budget is. Maybe you can only afford to spend $100 a month on clothes, that's fine. Whatever you want to buy with you $100 is whatever you buy! Whether you decide to find items at a thrift store, at a discounted store, or not doesn't matter. But, might I give you some advice on how to make your money go as far as possible?

Great, preciate that. If you aren't already, look for sales. Did you know even certain thrift stores have sales? Yeah, they can have different days with different percentages off. Don't pay full price for anything. I have a bad habit of wanting something and feeling like it won't be there later so I buy it full price, or I used to anyway. There's always a sale friend. Wait for it.

Don't just wait for sales though, do some comparison shopping. Check different places that sale similar items and see if you can find it cheaper. But y'all know all this right?

Back to variety! Get as many items as possible with your money that can add variety to your wardrobe. Not everything has to be a statement piece, make sure some things are the basics and can be used to maximum potential.

Of course there are plenty of people that will tell you to increase your income or decrease your bills in some way to make room for more money to spend on clothes. I'm not a financial advisor and all that is above my pay grade. The biggest thing I want you to know is: VARIETY. VARIETY. VARIETY. Options. Options. More options. The most important thing I want you to take away from this chapter isn't necessarily about where, when, why, or how you buy new clothes but rather how you take advantage of the clothes you buy. If you find it difficult to start seeing that variety in your clothes, find people on social media that have a different view on clothes than you and just watch what they do. There's nothing wrong with pulling inspiration from others, allowing your mind to be opened up to new ways of viewing something can always be beneficial.

It's A Mechanism, Not A Miracle

Being that my relationship with Jesus is the best relationship I've ever had, I do believe in miracles. That being said, I'm not trying to sell you a miracle in a book. I wish I could, and I'll believe with you if you're trusting God for a miracle, but I'm not trying to provide that here. Instead, this is just one of many mechanisms.

Coping mechanisms, not to be confused with defense mechanisms, are behaviors typically conscious and purposeful used to cope and handle significant life events. These are things we do to try to counteract stress and anxiety. Depending on the severity of where your mind is or how many triggers you have, you may have one or two coping mechanisms or you may have significantly more. It's important to note that not every mechanism will work the same for every situation.

For me, I have a number of coping mechanisms. One of the largest is style. I use style as an outlet and healthy expression of my emotions. I also read, write, and create. I also enjoy rewatching the same three crime shows over and over again, often starting from Season 1, Episode 1. These are just a few things I try to intentionally do to give myself the space to deal with wherever I am for whatever reason I am. Even outside of these, I dance in the mirror, exercise, and pray.

All of the shifting of your thoughts when considering your choice of style, especially for those who suffer from depression and anxiety, is just teaching you to do something with your mind to give everything time to catch up to itself.

I named a lot of coping mechanisms I have, right? They all play different parts for different reasons. Sometimes, I'll say, styling and putting an outfit together won't do it for me. I have to find something different. I may not actually have the get up and go to leave my house, much less shower and get dressed. So I may need to start with turning music on and doing my skincare routine. Maybe I just need to give myself a day to binge watch my favorite shows. Either way, I can't solely rely on just one mechanism to get me through.

Sure, as you begin to understand more about yourself and evaluate the coping mechanisms you have, you'll start to favor one that will work in most situations. That's what styling is for me. Most of the time it works, but let's be real sometimes life can be pretty spontaneous, even in the way it kicks our ass. There are a few things I want you to know about coping mechanisms. They are, in my opinion, liken to communication with yourself. They're about you trying to calm yourself down, cheer yourself up, offer your own pep talk, and dust yourself off. That being said, communication, with anyone, is something that evolves over time. As relationships progress, life happens, people grow, so does the way we communicate with others.

As you grow, and understand more about yourself, becoming more emotionally aware and intentional with your behavior, the things you need to say to yourself may change. How often you need to say certain things may change. That means that the mechanisms you use today may not be the same ones you use two years from now. Even if you are using the same thing, you may not be using it in the same capacity or way you are now. I know sometimes those of us who suffer with anxiety and depression can get a little confused, flustered, when we start to realize that things about us have changed and we missed it. I know how big the feelings can be feeling like you've become so detached from reality that you've missed a shift in yourself and now that you're aware you feel like you're lost at sea.

That's why I want to assure you that change is okay, and while sometimes it may be abrupt and obvious, it may also be gradual. It's okay if it changes over time.

There are many things I've mentioned through the course of this book that can be considered a mechanism. But y'know the crazy thing about this is that a mechanisms effectiveness can be personal to any given individual. What works extremely well for me may be counterproductive for you. Maybe just the idea of putting risky clothing items together sends you into a panic attack, in which case the mechanism of styling I benefit from would not be something to expect you to be able to benefit from. It does the opposite, and that's okay. For some reason, it seems we can be conditioned to be protective, even over the things we take the opportunity to vouch for, creating a potentially adverse reaction when someone tells us it didn't work for them. Something along the lines of, "You must not have done it right!" "Are you serious? You didn't know what you were doing." "You're just lazy."

Let's make abundantly clear that you may have read this entire book and try every little thing you could find from my words and none of it worked for you. Who am I to test the validity of your words? If you say it didn't work, it didn't work. Unless you are with a trained professional examining why some of these things may not be working, it doesn't matter what anyone else thinks. If it didn't work for you, that doesn't mean you're broken or a failure, it simply means you have to do something different than what the next person is doing.

What works for you may often change, adjust, refresh, and reset. All of that is okay, it's simply a part of your growth.

Let me also point out that when we think about miracles, we tend to think about something big happening quickly, immediately in some cases. Even if you consider the word mechanism, if you're thinking about it in a mechanical kind of way, that may seem like a quick process as well. Friend, lemme be clear: This is something to be worked at, it won't just happen over night.

Brick by Brick,
Not Building by Building

We've all heard John Haywood say, "Rome wasn't built in a day." Well friend, neither is your style. Or stability in your mental health for that matter. It's a growing process, a learning process, even a trying process. Everything about this is a roller coaster. Your mental health journey, your style journey, your self-care journey. All of these things will come with good days and bad, better days and worse. Much as is to be expected in life, sometimes more, sometimes less.

This is a brick by brick process, not building by building. What do I mean? Well lemme tell you friend. Buildings are much larger than a brick. And no matter how many different materials were used to build a building, it still took one piece of material after another to get the finished result. Layers and layers of this substance or that product to ensure the building was secure, safe, and fully functional. While some may look at big structures like shopping malls and centers and think that's exactly how it was built, building-by-building; that's the big picture of what a brick has the potential to be. Of course that's my opinion though.

Personally, I understand that if I focus on me, I'll be the best version of myself I can become. In that, I'll be doing every part that belongs to me in making things, people, and places around me better. That being said, I like focusing intimately on oneself, because at the end of the day you are the only one you have the power to fully control. In real life, when depression is big and anxiety is a massive wave, it's not the best time to focus on the biggest picture you can envision.

That tends to make the anxiety worse, increasing the gloomy feeling of failure or disappointment, keeping depression around longer. When I feel like I'm not connected to my body, as if my body is swimming through jello and my mind is absently bouncing from one thought to the next with periods of blank stares in between. These moments, I know it's a brick by brick moment. This means I could have to take it day by day for a while, maybe even hour by hour, sometimes it even has to be minute by minute. And that's okay. Sometimes things are rougher than others. Sometimes more things happen at once than we could prepare for.

When it comes to your style, anything could happen. You could gain weight, you could lose weight, you could get pregnant, you could find yourself not wanting to look the same anymore. The list of possible experiences is endless, making it even more imperative that you understand this is a slow and steady wins the race kind of process, like a 10k, not a 100-meter dash.

I know in the excitement of it all, we can get wrapped up in wanting to see the results immediately, but the reality is when it comes to both your style and your mental health, the results aren't something that can be rushed. The time put in working diligently on both of these areas is required for you to grow, consequently allowing your mental stability and style sense become more apparent.

The style you see in videos, the things I put together, the confidence I have when wearing it, I didn't just wake up one day and have all that. Actually, I take that back. There was one day where I just woke up and had it, but it came after many, many days crying, struggling, having to reconvince myself, having to let it play out good or bad. You aren't going to just throw all of your clothes away and go to the store and replace everything brand new in one day. You're not going to start seeing things exactly the way you eventually will when looking at something. It's a process that has to be worked.

When it comes to processes, it's interesting to consider that you have to make a conscious decision to keep working on the process. Whether you are on a new journey or in therapy, you have to commit to seeing the process through. You want to create something measureable at different intervals of the process to give yourself the ability to see if it's working or not.

Some things, like some of the coping mechanisms you'll try, may only take a couple times for you to know it's not going to work for you. But each time you decide that something doesn't work, that's not a stopping place, but a place of transition. Just because something doesn't work for you the way it worked for someone else doesn't mean anything is wrong with you. It just means you have to find what is going to fit whatever your needs are at the time. Either way, you want to make sure you give ample time to properly determine if something has the potential to work or not.

Every time I go to the doctor and they have to change a dosage or a prescription, I'm instructed to use it for a good three to six months depending on what it is. That's when the doctor is open to evaluating what the affects of said drug are on me based on what the goal was. Now, there have been times that I've known after the first dose, it wasn't going to work for me. But the majority of them, I'd at minimum have to give them two weeks to get in my system before I could even spot any difference one way or another. What does that tell you?

Give everything you try a little time. It took time to get where you are now, so it will take time for you to find what your thing is.

That being said, let's make sure we take a second to understand that your journey is unique to you. That means you can't look at when someone else you know is to determine if you're doing well or not. You can't look at my videos and try to measure your outfits to mine, I have been on a different journey than you, one unique to me. And as far as you know, I could be looking at someone else thinking the same. It can be an endless cycle of admiring what the next person has not appreciating what we hold in our own hands.

Friend, I don't care if you don't leave your house in that outfit for a year. If that's how long the process takes for you, I'm just proud you're still going. We tend to look at things like a daring race to the finish line, grasping to reach the end first, or at least not too far behind that people talk. How often are we taught to enjoy the process? I mean truly encouraged to enjoy the process, no matter what it looked like or how long it takes. We can see problems and want the fastest resolution, not considering the long lasting affects of the more temporal options we may choose. That's what I want you to start doing.

It may sound absolutely absurd right now, but why not just enjoy the process? What do you think could happen if you started to enjoy the growth process, leaning into the pains that come knowing that you will feel empowered, confident, and strong?

If you're into scripture, my favorite bible character is the Apostle Paul. Sure the testimony of who he was and who God called him to be was cool, but that part isn't why Paul made it to favorite bible character. Paul taught me how to enjoy the process of hardship. Now don't get me wrong, I'm not always as graceful as Paul seems to be throughout the New Testament. His entire life, after his name was changed, he experienced hardship after hardship, and then some more hardship for a little razzle dazzle. But his perspective concerning his suffering was always impeccable to me.

In my mind, I had unlocked the mystery of living at peace. Learning to find enjoyment in anything I had to go through. It wasn't the easiest perspective to adopt in the beginning, but with practice and years of redirecting my thoughts, I have truly come to a place where I enjoy the process, all of it. Of course I want to tap out sometimes, shoot sometimes I even do tap out. But that's far and few in between when I consider how much optimism I tend to show about the different things I face in life.

CPSIA information can be obtained
at www.ICGtesting.com
Printed in the USA
BVHW010408190422
634655BV00003B/13

9 781735 414034